THREE WORKS

Sedulius Scotus

Translated by: D.P. Curtin

Copyright @ 2007 Dalcassian Publishing Company

All rights reserved. No part of this publication may be reproduced, distributed, or transmitted in any form or by any means, including photocopying, recording, or other electronic or mechanical methods, without the prior written permission of the publisher, except in the case of brief quotations embodied in critical reviews and certain other non-commercial uses permitted by copyright law. For permission request, write to Dalcassian Publishing Company at dalcassianpublishing at gmail.com

ISBN: 979-8-8690-9227-4 (Paperback)

Library of Congress Control Number:
Author: Curtin, D.P. (1985-)

Printed by Ingram Content Group, 1 Ingram Blvd, La Vergne, Tennessee

First printing edition 2007.

Exhibitions on Genealogy

The difference between an argument and an argumentation is that an argument is the sense of the whole speech, whereas an argumentation is the expression of an argument and the explanation of it in competent words. But in the evangelical arguments this is particularly to be observed, that in them both the brevity of the speech and the clandestine subtlety of the senses are seen to sparkle; whence they rouse our dull intellect from the sleep of inactivity, and before the entrance of the evangelical doctrine make us more exercised and more awake, so that we may not walk lazily through the meadows of Sunday, perhaps with dry eyes, and with trembling feet of the senses, but with an enlightened mind, let us run through the flowery fields of Christ, with twinkling lamps before us. Indeed, what are the evangelical arguments, if not certain lamps coming from heavenly treasures and golden keys unlocking Sundays? Matthew from Judea, as he is placed first in the order, so he wrote the Gospel first in Judea. First of all, it should be noted that at the beginning of this argument, seven circumstances are highlighted, which are: person, thing or deed, cause, time, place, manner, matter. A person is recognized when the evangelist himself is referred to by his proper name Matthew: the race and origin of that person is shown when it is mentioned that the same Matthew was from Judea. Nor is the small amount of praise heaped upon the person of the preacher himself: for Matthew interprets the gifted, in that the Lord seven bestowed upon him the most important gifts: the first gift, faith; secondly, the apostleship; thirdly, virtues and miracles; fourthly, skill in languages; fifth, to write the Gospel; to be the sixth in order before the rest of the evangelists; seventh, to be crowned with the glory of martyrdom. It is to be noted that while the evangelist himself is said to have been from the tribe of Levi, here he is said to have been from Judea. This can be understood in three ways: either he arose from both tribes, Judah and Levi; or, although the lineage is not Jewish itself, yet it is asserted to have been from Judea, because perhaps his parents, as well as many from the tribe of Levi, dwelt there. Or if it is neither this nor that, from Judea the Jew is called συνεκδοχικῶς because all the Israelites are generally called Jews. The fact follows, this is the Gospel written by the same Matthew. The place of the event is described, when it is declared that the Gospel was written in Judea. The time of the writing of the Gospel is shown, when it is said that Matthew was the first to write his Gospel before the other evangelists. The cause of the act itself is made manifest when it is subjugated: whose call to God was from the acts of publicans. For this reason, he had written such a magnificent and divine work, because he had been chosen by the Lord for the apostleship from the works of publicans. Therefore, isolated from perverted acts, he was called by the Lord to an evangelical act. In which the manner or quality of the same fact is latently hinted at: for how or in what manner, if not orderly or truthfully, and if not wisely, did he write his Gospel, who was called and chosen by the true God, in whom are hidden all the treasures of wisdom and knowledge? Furthermore, the main material for the writing of the Gospel is shown when it is added: "assuming the principles of the two fathers in the generation of Christ." For he considered that the beginning of the Gospel should be taken from no other material than the genealogy of the Savior: so that while Christ was originally shown to be the son of two, that is, David and Abraham, he intimated that he was the one who had once been promised to both fathers. Abraham indeed, as: In thy seed shall all the tribes of the earth be blessed. And David said: Of the fruit of thy womb, I will put upon thy seat. And so that no one should doubt the merit of those two fathers, whose principles Matthew assumed in the genealogy of Christ, he immediately explains when he adds: "of one, whose first circumcision was in the flesh; of another, whose choice was according to his heart. From the preceding, that is, from that which is the beginning, by syllogism, the beginning must be assumed, and the participle ἀπὸ κοινοῦ, which is presuming, must be repeated, so that the sense is: of one, whose first circumcision in the flesh, presuming the beginning, of the other, whose second the heart was a choice, presuming the principle.

For what reason Matthew would place Abraham and David principally in the genealogy of the Savior, he shows by submitting, "and from both fathers is Christ." Indeed, Christ was born from both fathers, that is, Abraham and David, according to the flesh. For it was necessary that our Savior, who exists as the author of spiritual circumcision, by whose gift of faith we are circumcised from all sins, from Abraham, whose first circumcision was in the flesh by faith, should take his origin according to the flesh. And just as God was born of God according to divinity, so the king and son of God from King David, whose choice was according to his heart, would be born according to the flesh. And how many generations the genealogy of Christ is woven through many fathers, he directly enumerates below: "and the rest until: "a generation. It is easy to speak. For thus, that is, only with the two fathers Abraham and David placed at the front of the genealogy, 14 times, that is 42, generations are contained in Sunday's genealogy. And in the series itself a triple order is recognized. The first 14 generations from Abraham to David. The second 14 generations from David until the exile to Babylon. We will last from the transmigration of Babylon to Christ. But this number and order of time was not without a certain mystery explained by Matthew in the genealogy of Christ, whence it is submitted, "that he might satisfy both the number and the time." He satisfied himself with the number, while he placed fourteen generations three times in the genealogy itself; by which number both the decalogue of the law and the evangelical doctrine are expressed. He also satisfied the time, while Abraham placed the patriarch at the beginning of Sunday's genealogy. For the first age of the world, as a kind of childhood, extends from Adam to Noah. The second age, which is like the childhood of the world itself, is reckoned from Noah to Abraham. The third age, which is like the flowery youth of the world, extends from Abraham to King David, which indeed is considered an age suitable for procreation. Therefore, from Abraham, as if from the beginning of the world's youth, Matthew lists the generations in the genealogy of Christ in accordance, because the age itself seems suitable for the generation of offspring. It continues: "and so that he was showing, and the rest still: "he would not deny." For this reason, Matthew compiled the genealogy of Christ, so that he would not deny the testimony of Christ with his silent mouth. For he bears witness to Christ, while in the genealogy itself he testifies that he is the son of David and Abraham, and in addition he narrates his conception from the Holy Spirit, his birth from the Virgin, and other miracles of the same in his Gospel. Who Christ does many divine works not only in the apostles of the New Testament, with his coming, but from the beginning, that is, from the faith of believing, that is, from the time of Abraham, also in those patriarchs and prophets and righteous men, whose lineage Matthew has placed in the genealogy of Christ, in the signs and potentially worked miracles. Therefore, the holy evangelist does not deny bearing witness to Christ; but showing that he was, that is, that he was called by the Lord from the acts of the publicans and chosen to the apostleship, he shows that he has received the apostolic ministry, when he bears witness to the Savior. And the work of God, or the Gospel of Christ, shows in himself, while the Gospel itself was not only written in Hebrew letters, but also preached to others as a true apostle. It follows: "of which of all things," and the rest still: "God is Christ." That which he says: "it is necessary," must be joined to all things by syllemsin, so that there is a sense of which the time of all things is necessary. Order and number are also necessary. An arrangement or arrangement is necessary. But what is necessary for faith is that God is Christ. He therefore says all things, all that he had said above in this subject, this is that Matthew of Judaea was the first to write the gospel in Judaea, that he was called to God by the acts of the publicans, that two principles, that is He presupposed Abraham and David in the generation of Christ, and the rest of the like. For all these things the time is necessary, that is to say, in order to know the time at which these things took place. For example, from the time of Abraham the series of the genealogy of the Savior begins, and so on.

The order and number are clearly known in the above. The order in which Matthew is placed first in order before the other evangelists. Also, that he himself was first a publican, then called and chosen an apostle: nor is the order seen in the Savior's genealogy, when from Abraham to David, and from David in the time of the transmigration, and then to Christ, an ordered series of genealogy runs. The number is repeated three times, that is, it shines in 42 generations. Disposition, which is more significantly called ratio, is understood as the hidden and hidden cause of time itself, or of order or number. For when it is discussed in detail why from the time of Abraham to David, then from David to the transmigration, and from the transmigration to Christ, the time and order and number of forty-two generations are arranged in the genealogy of the Savior for the sake of mystery, this only arrangement or reason is mentioned. He says that all the above-mentioned things are necessary for all lovers of truth to know. But what is necessary for faith is God Christ, as if to say: If we know all the above-mentioned things about Christ, it is necessary that we firmly believe them by faith. And what is it that we ought to believe? It is true that God is Christ, that is, that the only begotten Son, who is true and eternal God according to his divinity, is also the same Christ, that is, he is anointed with the oil of joy before his fellows according to the humanity he has received. For Matthew shows this whole business in the genealogy of Christ. And how he who is true God according to divinity, Christ is man according to the flesh, he immediately explains, subsuming: "He who was made of woman," and the rest: "he fixed on the cross." For he who is the maker of all things according to his divinity, himself became man according to his participation in our frailty. But other men are made of both sexes; But he, who is the true God above men, became a true man, not from a man's seed, but from a woman conceived by the grace of the Spirit of God above. And he who, in the excellence of his divinity, is the supreme law above the law, became under the Mosaic law. And therefore, according to the law, he was circumcised on the eighth day. And because he says that he was made of a woman, so that no nuptial couple should be thought of in this, he consequently asserts that he was born of the virgin Mary. Who, while existing according to the impassive and immortal divinity, nevertheless, in order to deliver us from the passion and torture of eternal death, having suffered in the flesh, accepted a spontaneous death for us, fixing all our original and personal sins on the cross.

But you have heard the passage in the flesh, hear also the victory of the triumphant and the glory of the rising from hell. For it follows: "as triumphant in himself," and the rest still "in the children." He fixed everything, he says, on the cross, so that it might triumph, that is, conquering the sins and torments of sinners, and the demons themselves. For then he became triumphant, when, after his passion and death, he descended to the underworld. And this he did, not trusting in the strength of other heavenly or earthly men, but in himself.

When this triumph was accomplished, the glory of his resurrection followed. Therefore, rising in the body, he predestined all believers to eternal life, foreshadowed the hope of a glorious resurrection by his first resurrection. Thus the name of the supreme father among the fathers, that is, the pastors and teachers of the Church, restored to himself the Son as the head of the Church, for the glory of his name and his image. Just as the heavenly Father is a Father by nature, so by the gift of the same Father, the pastors of the Church, through the grace of the risen Son, are called spiritual Fathers. And just as the name of the supreme Father was given by the Son to the Fathers of the Catholic Church, who are called fathers by the gift of the Father from above, so also the name of the Son, in the many sons of the Church, was restored to the Father by the same only begotten Son. For through the passion, death, and resurrection of the Redeemer, both gifts were given to the Church, so that in the grace of the Father and the Son, many fathers and sons in the Church may become spiritual by the bounty of the heavenly gift. It continues: "without beginning, without end, showing that he is one with the Father because he is one." "It seems to be a brief conclusion of the superiors, as if it were to say plainly: When Christ was born of the Virgin, he suffered in the flesh, and fixed all his offenses on the cross, and triumphantly rose again in his own flesh in his own flesh, thus restoring the spiritual fathers and sons in the Church, and to these by all things done by none of the angels and men, but by the power of his divinity alone, he most evidently shows that he is one God with the Father. Not in the same way that carnal children are younger than their fathers in temporal space; but without beginning, without end, according to the eternal substance of the Godhead, God Himself is one with the Father. Why? Because he is one. Indeed, according to the nature of the Father, the Son is unique. For the rest of the sons are called sons of God, not by nature, but by adoption and grace. But here the Son is one by nature.

And so, after the passage of the Gospel period according to Matthew, it follows the whole argument of the anacephalous, that is, a recapitulation, by which the utility of the written Gospel is shown, "In which the Gospel is useful," and the rest: "let them review." In the Gospel itself, namely in evangelical doctrine, he asserts that there are three useful things to know. That is, it is either the first, or the middle, or the perfect: and what these first, middle, and perfect are, he directly explains, saying: "as both the calling of the apostle and the work of the

Gospel," and the rest. First, Matthew was called by the Lord from the acts of the tax collector to be an apostle. Secondly, the Gospel of Christ was written by the same person, in which the gift of the perfect love of God born in the flesh towards the human race, through all the words and deeds of the Lord, can be understood by anyone who reads with interest. Thus in the same Gospel the very gift of charity in which they have been apprehended and chosen by God, they themselves seek to apprehend God, the source of love, with all the ardor of their minds, by reading and searching. Although the first, the middle, and the perfect can be understood differently, that is, everything that is useful, more useful, and most useful in evangelical doctrine. As, for example, marriage, widowhood, and virginity, which are allegorically signified by the thirtieth, sixtieth, and hundredth fruit. Otherwise, the first are those which are told in the Gospel from the Lord's conception [Cod. and reception of God] until his baptism. The means which are contained in the same Gospel from baptism to the imminent time of passion. Perfect, which are recorded in the last parts of the Gospel about his passion, death and resurrection. It continues: "For us this was in the study of the argument," and the rest: "not to be silent." Because the argument is a prayer, making the belief of a doubtful matter, we have composed this argument for two reasons. The first reason is that we would point out in a short speech, from the genealogy of the Savior to the same triumph of the resurrection, the faith, that is, the simple truth of the things that happened, that is, of each of the events narrated in the Gospel by Matthew, summarizing this argument. The second reason is that we should not be silent about it, but rather remind the readers of this topic, that in all that is narrated in the Gospel about the words and deeds of Dominic, the wonderful disposition of the working God must be carefully understood by certain pious people and those who desire God. For in arguments both are necessary, so that the faith of the matter of doubt is made, and a certain understanding of things is shown, because faith's understanding of the things done is necessary: for it is not enough to believe, unless what is believed is also understood.

It is explicit in the argument according to Matthew.

Explanatiuncula on the difference between the breviaries, chapters, and the canons

The Abbreviation of the second chapter of Matthew begins with the Nativity of Christ, and Magi who came with gifts, and so on.

We must inquire what is the difference between the breviary and the chapter and the canon. Indeed, with these three, as if with certain keys, all the mysteries of the Gospel volume are unlocked. For when the breviaries, chapters, and canons are taken away, everything will be confused and ambiguous, and what is the same, or neighboring, or alone, and who or how many evangelists agree in any sentences, or about what things they had published, all this will be amphibole without the aforesaid keys. And so let us distinguish these three from one another by their proper differences. A brief is a concise and brief exposition of the things narrated in the context of the Gospel. Hence it is called a breviary for a short reason, because by this means the whole text of the Gospels is briefly comprehended. A chapter is any sentence or narrative in the Gospels. Canon is the title by which the agreement of the evangelists is known, that is, who, or who, or how many evangelists published each chapter. For these three reasons, therefore, they were discovered. For the breviary was discovered for this reason, inasmuch as the very things which are narrated in the evangelical volume, by this summary briefly prefaced and considered, appear more quickly and clearly, so that what everyone wishes to find in the Gospel, he finds with the greatest ease by considering the breviaries. Canons were found and called for this reason, insofar as their distinction, the agreement of the evangelists, that is, who and how many evangelists said the same or adjacent or single chapters in the Gospels, is recognized. Chapters were invented and marked for this reason, so that every sentence or narrative in every Gospel can be recognized by them. It should also be noted that neither a chapter without a canon, nor a canon without a chapter, can be the context of the whole Gospel, because these two are inseparably connected with each other. For although it may happen that, due to the negligence of the writers, any chapter does not have the number of its canon subscribed to it, yet it cannot really be without some canon. But the breviary stands without canon or subscribed chapters, although not without the meaning of the chapters. For it is not in the breviary who or how many evangelists published in any sense, nor the number of chapters: otherwise, how would the context of the evangelical, so also in the breviary, each number of canons and chapters be added by overwriting. Since this is not discussed, it is clear that it is properly learned in the breviary, so that what is set forth in a multiple narrative in different chapters and canons in the evangelical text, those are shown in the breviary, as if in a kind of punch, by a short statement.

It should also be noted that just as the breviary stands without the canon and the chapters, so the chapters are often found without the breviary. For in the beginning of the Gospel according to Matthew, in which 14, that is, 42 generations are described three times, two chapters and two canons, namely the third and tenth canon, are included without the breviary. If, indeed, in what follows, the generation of Christ was thus, and the rest, the beginning of the breviary begins. For there the Nativity of the Lord is set forth. But why the breviary of the Gospel according to Matthew does not begin at the beginning of the 40th and two generations, must be investigated. For such a breviary could, without any objectionable reason, thus be seen, enumerate 40 two generations, the birth of Christ, and the rest: but because of the excellence of Sunday's nativity, he took the beginning of the breviary from the last, that is, the forty-second generation, or the birth of the Savior. Nor is it surprising that in a breviary, just as certain things are collected in a breviary, so some are omitted for the sake of brevity, since both are proper to the breviary: otherwise, a breviary would not be a breviary. It should also be noted in the other evangelists that in these certain chapters and canons are found placed before the beginning of the breviary, just as in the beginnings of the Gospels of Mark, Luke and John, after certain chapters or canons, the beginnings of the breviaries begin. It must also be known that while the canons and chapters are recorded, sometimes at the beginning, sometimes in the middle, sometimes even near the end of each sense, the breviaries only begin in the primordial places of the senses. Hence it happens that the breviaries themselves often begin at the beginning, sometimes in the middle, sometimes even near the end of the chapters, but still at the beginning of the senses.

Explanations on Mark's Episcopacy

This argument clarifies the type and office and election of Mark the evangelist in the first part, the second shows the intention of the same evangelist in writing the Gospel of Christ, the third describes the dignity of the episcopate of Mark himself with a proclamation of praise. Finally, he reminds us how we should understand the evangelical work itself. Accordingly, the name and office of the person himself is placed at the front of the argument, when Mark the evangelist himself is designated. "Mark the evangelist:" Mark in the Hebrew language is called exalted; evangelist is translated from the Greek word for good news. "A son of God and Peter in baptism, and a disciple in the divine discourse." Because of this he merited to become an exalted and evangelist, because by divine grace he was first reborn in baptism in Christ and was instructed in divine wisdom. And so it must be distinguished, that first it is pronounced "Mark the evangelist," and then it is subsumed: "The son of God and Peter in baptism." Mark is the son of God in baptism, because he is reborn in God at the source of baptism, through the grace of adoption he becomes the Son of God. Peter's son is said to be in baptism, because being baptized and instructed by him, he is rightly called his spiritual son. On which subject the Apostle says: My children, whom I will give birth to again until Christ is formed in you. "A Levite acting as a priest in Israel according to the flesh." "The former priestly office and carnal nobility of the lineage of the same Mark is shown, so that he did not undeservedly transcend to the summit of a spiritual and more excellent priesthood, who had previously exercised the carnal priesthood justly and legitimately in Israel, when he arose from the priestly tribe of Levi. But when and where he wrote the Gospel is shown when it is submitted: "He converted to the faith of Christ and wrote the Gospel in Italy." Then, he says, he wrote the Gospel, after he had been converted to the faith of Christ. For before he perceived the faith of Christ, he could not write worthy of Christ. The place of the writing of the Gospel is shown to be Italy, in which the work itself is said to have been written: not that it was written in Italian or Roman, but in Greek.

But why Mark wrote the Gospel is shown when it is subjoined: "Showing in that work what he owed to his race and to Christ." For since he himself was a

Levite, from which tribe many prophets had sprung, he duly began his Gospel with a prophetic voice: and as a Levite, John the Baptist was likewise a Levite and prophet of the Most High, he himself had to bear witness with a prophetic voice. Moreover, when Christ took the origin of the flesh not only from the tribe of Judah, but also from the tribe of Levi, the evangelist Leviticus was indebted to the Lord himself to write down his Gospel. Whence it is submitted: "for establishing the beginning of the beginning in the voice of the prophetic exclamation, he shows the order of the Levitical election." "For it is clear that blessed Mark demonstrated the due service of the Levites in evangelical work, while he did not manage to arrange the beginning of his Gospel anywhere else than in prophetic speeches, and like a good worker and architect he began to build the evangelical work on the foundation of the prophets: not that the prophets did not arise from other tribes , but because the prophetic ministry had been granted mainly to the Levitical tribe according to the election of the Lord. It was not, therefore, as if by robbery that Marcus usurped a ministry which was not due to him, but in accordance with the choice of his lineage he began to write the Gospel. What he says, "the beginning of the beginning," is difficult to understand. For the discoverer of this argument could have said more commonly: the beginning of the Gospel, or the beginning of the Gospel: but he chose to speak more abstrusely than usual. It must therefore be known that there is this distance between the principle and the beginning, because the principle includes several sentences in itself, but the beginning is a part of the principle, that is, every main sentence enclosed within the principle itself. Therefore, the beginning of the Gospel according to Mark, let us understand all that is reported in the four main chapters about John the Baptist. But that the beginning is the beginning of the beginning itself, that is the prophetic prophecy which had once been foretold concerning John himself, the forerunner of the Lord; this is that an angel is set before the face of the Lord, and the voice of the Father precedes the word. The reason why Mark should begin in the voice of the prophetic exclamation, the beginning of the very beginning, is shown when it is submitted: "that he might show the predestined John the son of Zacharias" and the rest: While blessed Mark preaches John, the forerunner of the Lord, that the angel is before the face, that is, the manifest appearance of the incarnation of Christ, preceded, and that the voice is the word of the Father, in conception, birth, teaching, baptism, running ahead, there is no doubt that not only the Word, that He is the only Son of God, shows that he took flesh, but also declares that he had a true soul inseparably.

For not according to heretical perversion, the divinity of Christ assumed only flesh without a soul, but the whole man according to body and soul. But in what he says, "the body of the Lord was animated in all things by the word of the divine voice," we must understand there no other word than the divine voice, so that there is a sense, by the word of the divine voice, by the word itself, which is nothing else than the divine voice. For the word of the Father is the same and the voice. of the Father, by whose word all things were made, so the soul of Christ was created. For this reason, it is said: "the body of the Lord was animated in all things by the word of the divine voice." "Therefore, having heard the name of a word or a voice, we are not disturbed by carnal habit, so that we think of such a word or voice of the Father, as we utter sounding and transitory words. But we shall notice this better in what follows.

For it is submitted. "That he who reads these things may know to whom," and the rest, "may find." The order of the words is: That he who reads these things may know, who ought to know and preach, to recognize the beginning of the flesh in the Lord, and the flesh, that is the habitation of the coming Jesus; and he would find that word of the voice which he had lost in the consonants of the other evangelists. It was fitting, he says, that Marcus the Levite should write about the Lord the Savior, who was born from Levi, so that anyone who reads these things will know the leadership, order and a certain privilege of the Levitical election. For what more appropriate than the flesh of the Levites, that is, the carnal lineage and origin, should have acknowledged the beginning of the taking of flesh in the Lord or in the unity of the Lord's person? What is the flesh of the Savior, what else is there to be said than that of Jesus coming into this world as a dwelling place, who was found in the habit of flesh as a man? For those evangelists who sprang from Levi, such as Matthew and Mark, were more worthy than the rest to write the mystery of the incarnation of the Lord, who also sprang from Levi. It was also fitting that the same Levitical flesh, or Mark, who had carnal origin from the tribe of Levi, should find in himself, that is, in his mind and intellect, the word of the voice. Wherein we must note that although John the Baptist is called the voice, and Christ the word, yet Christ is not the voice or John, but rather the Word of the Father or the Son. We can, however, say that Jesus himself is the word of the voice, and Jesus is inconsistently called the word of John, who is called the voice, because he preached the Word or Christ before him. For we can say the word of the voice, the word or the discourse which the voice speaks. Not that John begat that word, but that, as a voice, he preceded the Word himself, or Christ, by prophesying. For who doubts that our voice first sounds, that afterwards the word may be heard?

And that which he says, "which he had lost in the consonants," seems to be an inextricable knot. For if the maker of this argument were to say that he had revealed the consonants, so that there was a sense that Mark had revealed this word of the voice, or the speech of John, even to other evangelists who were consonant with Mark, it would be an easy understanding. But since he had not betrayed but lost, it is written in the copies, we must inquire how Mark lost this word of the voice in the consonants of the other evangelists. Or perhaps he had not found this word of speech in them, so that this is to lose what it is not to find? For it is certain that the mystery of the incarnation of Christ was understood by Marcus, the disciple of Peter the apostle, both from prophetic and apostolic teaching. However, he did not find the word of the divine voice, or Christ, according to his deity, the Word of the Father, shown in the consonantal evangelists, or in Matthew and Luke, who according to some, as ecclesiastical history says, wrote his Gospels before Mark, for this mystery of the word must sometimes be shown only John had been reserved as a higher flying eagle. And when Mark had found the voice of one crying, that is, John, said to be a voice, also in harmony with the other evangelists, he found Christ also the word of the voice, although not in the writings of others, yet in himself, that is, in his own mind, beyond doubt. Therefore, although Mark had found in the consonantal evangelists, or Matthew and Luke, that John himself was called by the name of the voice, yet he had not read the word of the voice, or the only Son of God, designated by the name of the Word, in the consonantal evangelists, while not yet blessed John had shown the secret mystery of the Word itself in the writings ; that, however, Marcus had undoubtedly found the Word in himself, that is, in his understanding, by divine revealing grace. For the holy evangelist, who was the chosen temple of God, did not hide the mystery of the word of the divine voice, although he had not learned this word from the writings of other evangelists.

It continues: "Finally, entering into the work of the finished Gospel," and the rest: "He brought forth the angels." "The perfect gospel is said to have been preached by the Lord himself for three and a half years after the baptism received by John until the time of his passion and resurrection. Accordingly, Mark is designated by the form of a man, when he narrated briefly what the man Christ had done in the flesh, omitting the mystery of the Word, which is Christ, and acknowledging that the genealogy of the flesh was fully described in the earlier evangelists, that is, in Matthew and Luke. The whole is therefore said to be either full or perfect, because he reported full and perfect from the Lord. It is said in the first, or in the principal passages of his Gospel: for he did not bring forth the whole in all, in the middle or in the last passages, when in some he omitted many things in their entirety, but in the first he told all these things briefly; viz., the exposition of the wilderness, the fasting of the number, the temptation of the devil, the gathering of beasts, and the ministry of angels. Where it is to be noted why the fast is the number, and not rather the number of the fast, except because the number is more prominent than the fast. For the number was not because of the fast, but because of the sacred number, that fast had been completed for so many days and nights. For the number of forty contains a great mystery in itself, and from this the fasting of its own right is the number of forty itself. But why did he bring all these things forward? He said, "In order to instruct us to understand," and the rest: "He would not deny it." For it was fitting that he should confine, as it were, every action of the Sunday in a short pocketbook or tablet, for as nothing is more tedious than long-windedness, so nothing is more agreeable than clear brevity. In order not to lose the authority of what has been done. He mentions the authority of the authorial magisterium, by which Marcus had been instructed by the mouth of Peter the apostle concerning the sayings and deeds of Dominic. Therefore, just as from the teaching of Peter the Apostle he learned the history of the actual event, that is, of the action of Dominic, so skimming, as the Holy Spirit guided his understanding, he delivered the same history in letters, and yet he had not lost anything of what he had written, by keeping silent and concealing it. Thus, in completing his evangelical work, he did not deny the fullness of it, while he completed the full work of all that he had begun to write, albeit in a short speech.

Therefore, let us pay attention to the fact that Mark was chosen for the evangelical work by divine predestination, and that the Lord's predestination cannot be prevented on any occasion. "Finally, it is said that he amputated his thumb after faith," and the rest goes on: "He was a bishop." It had been the custom of the Hebrew people that no one having a dishonorable spot on his body should reach the priesthood. By which it is mystically insinuated that no one contaminated by the stains of sins is worthy of the priesthood. Mark, following the letter, cut off his thumb because of his humility, so that he would not ascend to the summit of a better priesthood as if he had already been reprobate. But in the very fact that he considered himself unworthy of the priesthood, he became more worthy. For according to the divine predestination there existed not as a priest or a doctor, but also the bishop of the most illustrious city of Alexandria, so that he who had written the Gospel in the Greek language, might minister to the Greeks who lived there and to all the nations of Africa, as if on a waterless land, the flow of divine dogmas.

Having explained these, a brief conclusion of the argument is submitted: "whose work we need to know in detail," and the rest: "we want to be recognized." » To all these sentences the word that we want must be attached by means of a zeugma. That there may be a sense whose work we wish to know in detail, and that we wish to arrange the sayings of the Gospel in ourselves, and that we wish to understand the divine nature in the flesh of God, which we wish first to be required of us, and afterwards we wish to be recognized by inquiry. But what he says is that we recognize the discipline of the law in Mark, and we do not inconsistently accept both the prophetic sentences and the testimonies taken from the divine law, wherever they are introduced in the Gospel of Mark. For the Mosaic law, prophecy, and psalm are often designated by the name of the law. And so, the discoverer of this argument hopes to receive a reward for his labor, thus subjoining: "having the reward of exhortation: he who plants and he who waters are one, but he who ensures growth is God." The apostle writes of this sense in this way: I planted, Apollo watered, but God gave the increase. The apostle plants, while he labors at rooting faith in Sunday's vineyard, or in Christ's Church: but Apollos, both by baptism and by the subsequent doctrine of exhortation, waters them: yet God gives the increase of faith to his faithful. Therefore, both the one who plants and the one who waters are one, because they believe the same thing, they desire the same thing: if indeed they desire to grasp the truth by searching, discovering, exhorting, and teaching. One of whom was the discoverer of this argument.

It ends in an argument according to Mark.

LATIN TEXT

Expositiuncula

Inter argumentum et argumentationem hoc distat quod argumentum est sensus totius orationis, argumentatio vero est argumenti elocutio verbisque competentibus explicatio. In argumentis autem evangelicis hoc praecipue attendendum est quod in his et sermonis brevitas, et sensuum clandestina subtilitas scintillare cernitur; unde nostrum torpens ingenium ex inertiae somno suscitant, et ante introitum doctrinae evangelicae nos exercitatiores evigilantioresque reddunt, ne lippidulis fortasse oculis, pedibusque sensuum titubantibus, prata Dominica segniter incedamus, sed illustrata mentis acie florida Christi rura, coruscis praecedentibus lucernis, percurramus. Quid etenim sunt argumenta evangelica, nisi quaedam coelestium thesaurorum provenientes lampades simul et aureae claves gazas reserantes Dominicas? Matthaeus ex Judaea, sicut in ordine primus ponitur, ita Evangelium in Judaea primus scripsit. Primo notandum quod in hujus argumenti exordio, VII circumstantiae elucent, quae sunt: persona, res vel factum, causa, tempus, locus, modus, materia. Persona dignoscitur, cum ipse evangelista proprio nomine Matthaeus nominatur: cujus personae gens et origo ostenditur, cum idem Matthaeus ex Judaea fuisse commemoratur. Nec parvae quoque laudis praeconium ipsi personae cumulatur: Matthaeus namque donatus interpretatur, in eo quod ei Dominus VII praecipua dona largitus fuerit: primum donum, fidem; secundum, apostolatum; tertium, virtutes atque miracula; quartum, linguarum peritiam; quintum, Evangelium scribere; sextum ante caeteros evangelistas primum esse in ordine; septimum, martyrii gloria coronari. Notandum vero est quod cum ipse evangelista ex tribu Levi fuisse tradatur, hic ex Judaea fuisse refertur. Quod tripliciter intelligi poterit: aut enim ex utraque tribu et Juda et Levi ortus est; aut, licet prosapia non sit ipse Judaeus, tamen ex Judaea fuisse asseritur, eo quod forte parentes ejus, quomodo et multi ex Levi tribu, ibidem habitaverunt. Aut si neque hoc est neque illud, ex Judaea Judaeus ob hoc συνεκδοχικῶς nominatur, eo quod omnes Israelitae generaliter Judaei appellantur. Sequitur factum, hoc est Evangelium ab eodem Matthaeo conscriptum. Locus facti describitur, cum illud Evangelium in Judaea fuisse scriptum declaratur. Tempus Evangelli conscribendi ostenditur, cum is Matthaeus primus ante alios evangelistas suum Evangelium scripsisse perhibetur. Causa ipsius facti manifestatur, cum subjungitur: cujus vocatio ad Deum ex publicanis actibus fuit. Idcirco enim tam magnificum divinumque opus scripserat, quia ex publicanis operibus in apostolatum a Domino electus erat. Itaque a perversis actibus segregatus, ad actum evangelicum a Domino fuit vocatus. In quo et modus seu qualitas ejusdem facti latenter insinuatur: quomodo enim vel qualiter, nisi ordinate vel veraciter, nisique sapienter suum Evangelium conscripserit, qui a vero Deo, in quo sunt omnes thesauri sapientiae et scientiae absconditi, vocatus atque electus fuit? Porro principalis materia conscribendi Evangelii ostenditur, cum subinfertur: « duorum patrum in generatione Christi principia praesumens. » Non enim ab alia materia, nisi a Salvatoris genealogia, exordium Evangelii sumendum esse censuit: ut dum Christum filium et duorum id est, David et Abraham, originaliter ostenderet, ipsum esse intimaret qui utrisque patribus quondam promissus fuerat. Abrahae quidem, ut: In semine tuo benedicentur omnes tribus terrae. David vero: De fructu ventris tui ponam super sedem tuam. Ac ne quis dubitaret quanti meriti sint illi duo patres, quorum principia Matthaeus in genealogia Christi praesumpsit, continuo exponit cum subdit: « unius, cujus prima circumcisio in carne; alterius, cujus secundum cor electio fuit. » Ex praecedentibus, id est ab eo quod est principia, per syllemsim, principium assumendum est, atque ἀπὸ κοινοῦ participium, quod est praesumens, repetendum est, ut sit sensus: unius, cujus prima circumcisio in carne, principium praesumens, alterius, cujus secundum cor electio fuit, principium praesumens.

Ob quam vero causam Matthaeus Abraham et David in genealogia Salvatoris principaliter poneret, ostendit subdens « et ex utrisque patribus Christus. » Siquidem Christus ex utroque patre, id est Abraham et David, secundum carnem exortus est. Oportebat enim ut Salvator noster, qui spiritualis circumcisionis auctor existit, cujus fidei dono nos ab omnibus peccatis circumcidimus, ex Abraham, cujus prima circumcisio per fidem in carne fuit, secundum carnem originem duceret. Et quomodo Deus de Deo natus est secundum divinitatem, ita et rex filiusque Dei ex David rege, cujus secundum cor electio fuit, nasceretur secundum carnem. Quot autem generationibus genealogia Christi in multis patribus contexitur, protinus enumerat subdens: « sicque quaternario denario numero triformiter posito; » et reliqua usque: « generationem. » Facile est quod proloquitur. Nam sic, id est tantum duobus patribus Abraham et David in fronte genealogiae antepositis, ter XIV, id est XLII, generationes in Dominica genealogia continentur. Atque in ipsa serie triplex ordo dignoscitur. Primus XIV generationes ab Abraham usque ad David. Secundus XIV generationes a David usque ad transmigrationem Babylonis. Postremus a transmigratione Babylonis usque ad Christum. Sed hunc numerum ac temporis ordinem non sine certi mysterii ratione Matthaeus in Christi genealogia digessit, unde subditur, « ut et numero satisfaceret, et tempori. » Numero satisfecit, dum ter XIV generationes in ipsa genealogia posuit; quo numero et decalogus legis et evangelica doctrina exprimitur. Tempori quoque satisfecit, dum Abraham patriarcham in exordio Dominicae genealogiae posuit. Nam prima mundi aetas, quasi quaedam infantia, ab Adam usque Noe protenditur. Secunda aetas, quae est veluti ipsius mundi pueritia, a Noe usque ad Abraham computatur. Tertia aetas, quae est quasi florida mundi adolescentia, ab Abraham usque ad David regem extenditur, quae quidem aetas habilis ad generandum habetur. Ideoque ab Abraham, quasi ab exordio adolescentiae mundi, Matthaeus ipsas generationes in genealogia Christi congruenter enumerat, quia ipsa aetas ad generandam sobolem apta esse videtur. Sequitur: « et sic quod esset ostendens, et reliqua usque: « non negaret. » Ob hoc praecipue genealogiam Christi Matthaeus contexuit, ut non ore tacito negaret testimonium Christi. Nam testimonium perhibet de Christo, dum in ipsa genealogia ipsum filium David et Abrahae esse testatur, et praeterea conceptionem ejus de Spiritu sancto, et nativitatem ex Virgine, et caetera ejusdem miracula in suo Evangelio narrat. Qui Christus non solum in apostolis Novi Testamenti, suo adventu multa divina operatur, sed a principio, id est a credendi fide, hoc est ab Abrahae tempore, etiam in his patriarchis et prophetis et justis, quorum genus in Christi genealogia Matthaeus posuit, in signis et miraculis potentialiter operatus est. Sanctus itaque evangelista testimonium perhibere de Christo non denegat; sed quod esset ostendens, id est, quod a Domino ex publicanis actibus vocatus sit atque in apostolatum electus, ostendit se apostolicum ministerium accepisse, cum testimonium perhibet de Salvatore. Et Dei opus vel Evangelium Christi in se demonstrat, dum ipsum Evangelium non solum Hebraicis litteris scripserit, sed etiam ut verus apostolus aliis praedicavit. Sequitur: « quarum omnium rerum, » et reliqua usque: « Deus Christus est. » Illud quod ait: « necessarium est, » per syllemsin ad omnia conjungendum est ut sit sensus, quarum omnium rerum tempus necessarium est. Ordo quoque et numerus necessarius est. Dispositio vel ratio necessaria est. Quod autem fidei necessarium est, Deus Christus est Omnes itaque res dicit, cuncta quae superius in hoc argumento dixerat, hoc est, quod Matthaeus ex Judaea primus in Judaea evangelium scripserit, quod a publicanis actibus ad

Deum vocatus sit, quod duo principia, id est Abraham et David in generatione Christi praesumpserit, et reliqua consimilia. Quarum omnium rerum tempus necessarium est, id est ad dignoscendum quo tempore haec gesta sunt. Ut, verbi gratia, a tempore Abraham series genealogiae Salvatoris exordium sumit, caeteraque consimilia.

Ordo quoque et numerus in supra dictis evidenter cognoscuntur. Ordo, quod Matthaeus in ordine primus ante alios evangelistas ponitur. Item quod ipse prius publicanus, dehinc vocatus atque electus sit apostolus: nec non et ordo in genealogia Salvatoris cernitur, cum ab Abraham usque ad David atque a David in transmigrationis tempus, dehinc usque ad Christum, ordinata genealogiae series percurrit. Numerus in ter replicatur, id est in XLII generationibus elucescit. Dispositio, quae significantius ratio nominatur, abdita et occulta causa ipsius temporis vel ordinis seu numeri intelligitur. Nam cum subtiliter discutitur cur a tempore Abraham usque ad David, dehinc a David ad transmigrationem, atque a transmigratione usque ad Christum, tempus et ordo ac numerus XLII generationum, in genealogia Salvatoris causa mysterii disponitur, hoc solum dispositio vel ratio nominatur. Quae prorsus omnia supradicta omnibus veritatis amatoribus ad cognoscendum dicit esse necessaria. Quod autem fidei necessarium est, Deus Christus est, ac si dicat: Si omnia supradicta de Christo cognoscimus, necessarium est ut ea per fidem firmiter credamus. Quod est autem quod credere debeamus? Illud profecto quod Deus Christus est, id est, quod unigenitus Filius, qui verus et aeternus Deus est secundum divinitatem, idem quoque Christus, id est, unctus sit oleo laetitiae prae participibus suis secundum susceptam humanitatem. Nam hoc totum negotium in genealogia Christi Matthaeus ostendit. Quomodo autem qui verus Deus est secundum divinitatem, Christus homo sit secundum carnem, continuo explanat subdens: « qui factus est ex muliere, » et reliqua usque: « in cruce fixit. » Nam qui omnium factor est secundum divinitatem, ipse homo factus est secundum nostrae fragilitatis participationem. Sed caeteri homines ex utroque sexu fiunt; ipse vero, qui supra homines verus Deus est, non ex virili semine, sed de superna Spiritus Dei gratia conceptus ex muliere verus homo est factus. Et qui suae divinitatis excellentia, summa lex supra legem est, sub lege Mosaica factus est. Ideoque quasi legi subditus octavo die circumcisus est. Et quia ex muliere eum dicit esse factum, ne ulla nuptialis copula in hoc cogitetur, ipsum ex virgine Maria natum esse consequenter asserit. Qui dum secundum divinitatem impassibilis et immortalis existat, tamen ut nos ab aeternae mortis passione et cruciatu eriperet, passus in carne, spontaneam pro nobis mortem susceperat, omnia nostra et originalia et propria peccata in cruce figens.

Sed audisti passum in carne, audi quoque victoriam triumphantis gloriamque ab inferis resurgentis. Nam sequitur: « ut triumphans ea in semetipso, » et reliqua usque « in filiis. » Omnia, inquit, in cruce fixit, ut triumpharet ea, scilicet peccata peccatorumque tormenta, ipsaque daemonia vincens. Tunc enim triumphator factus est, cum post passionem suam et mortem ad inferos descendens, ipsum qui habebat mortis imperium sua morte detraxit, atque captivam captivitatem ad superos secum eduxit. Hoc autem fecit, non in aliorum coelestium vel terrestrium confidens fortitudine, sed in semetipso. Quo triumpho peracto, gloria resurrectionis est ejus subsecuta. Unde ipse resurgens in corpore cunctis credentibus ad vitam aeternam praedestinatis, spem gloriae resurrectionis sua prima resurrectione praemonstravit. Sicque nomen summi patris in patribus, id est, Ecclesiae pastoribus et doctoribus, sibi Filio quasi capiti Ecclesiae, ad sui nominis gloriam suamque ad imaginem restituens. Ut quomodo coelestis Pater natura sit Pater, sic ejusdem Patris dono, pastores Ecclesiae, per Filii resurgentis gratiam, spirituales Patres nominentur. Quomodo autem nomen Patris summi, catholicae Ecclesiae Patribus qui dono superni genitoris patres nominantur, per Filium donatum est, sic et nomen Filii, in multis Ecclesiae filiis, per eumdem unigenitum Filium Patri restitutum est. Nam per Redemptoris passionem mortemque ac resurrectionem, utrumque donum Ecclesiae collatum est, ut in Patris et Filii gratiam, multi tam patres quam filii in Ecclesia spirituales superni muneris largitione fiant. Sequitur: « sine principio, sine fine, ostendens unum se cum Patre esse quia unus est. » Brevis superiorum conclusio esse videtur, ac si aperte dicat: Cum Christus ex Virgine sit natus, passus in carne, omniaque delicta in cruce fixit, atque ea triumphans in semetipso propria in carne gloriose resurrexit, sicque spirituales patres et filios in Ecclesia restituit, hisque omnibus a nullo angelorum hominumque sed sola suae divinitatis potentia gestis, evidentissime ostendit unum Deum se cum Patre esse. Non quomodo carnales filii temporali spatio suis patribus sunt aetate minores; sed sine principio, sine fine, secundum aeternam divinitatis substantiam, unus ipse Deus est cum Patre. Quare? Quia unus est. Siquidem unicus est secundum naturam Patris filius. Nam caeteri filii non natura, sed adoptione et gratia, filii Dei nominantur. Hic vero unus est natura Filius.

Itaque decursa secundum Matthaeum Evangelii periocha, sequitur totius argumenti anacephaleosis, id est recapitulatio, qua conscripti Evangelii utilitas ostenditur « In quo Evangelio utile est, » et reliqua usque: « recognoscant. » In ipso Evangelio, in doctrina scilicet evangelica, tria quaedam utilia esse ad cognoscendum asserit. Id est vel prima, vel media, vel perfecta: et quae sunt illa prima, media et perfecta, protinus exponit dicens: « ut et vocationem apostoli et opus Evangelii, » et reliqua. Primo namque Matthaeus ex publicanis actibus a Domino vocatus est ut esset apostolus. Secundo Christi Evangelium ab eodem est conscriptum, in quo prorsus opere donum perfectae dilectionis Dei in carne nascentis erga humanum genus, per universa dicta et facta Dominica, quilibet studiose legentes intelligere possunt. Sicque in eodem Evangelio ipsum charitatis donum in quo a Deo apprehensi sunt atque electi, ipsique toto mentis ardore Deum fontem dilectionis apprehendere expetunt, legendo et perscrutando recognoscant. Licet et aliter prima et media et perfecta intelligi possunt, id est quaeque in doctrina evangelica, utilia, utiliora atque utilissima. Ut, verbi gratia, conjugium, viduitas, virginitas, quae per tricesimum et sexagesimum atque centesimum fructum allegorice designantur. Aliter prima sunt ea quae in Evangelio a conceptione Domini [Cod., ac receptione Deum] usque ad ejus baptismum narrantur. Media, quae a baptismo usque ad imminens passionis tempus in eodem Evangelio continentur. Perfecta, quae in ultimis Evangelii partibus de ejus passione morteque ac resurrectione conscribuntur. Sequitur: « nobis enim hoc in studio argumenti fuit, » et reliqua usque: « non tacere. » Quia argumentum est oratio, rei dubiae faciens fidem, ob duas causas hoc argumentum composuimus. Prima causa est ut nos factae, id est, cujuslibet gestae rei, et in Evangelio per Matthaeum narratae, fidem, hoc est, simplicem veritatem rerum gestarum, brevi sermone a genealogia Salvatoris usque ad ejusdem triumphum resurrectionis, summatim hoc argumento monstraremus. Secunda causa est ut illud non taceremus, sed potius lectores hoc argumento admoneremus, quod in omnibus quae in Evangelio de dictis et factis Dominicis narrantur, operantis Dei mirabilis dispositio a piis quibusdam Deumque desiderantibus diligenter intelligenda sit. Nam in argumentis utrumque necessarium est ut et fides rei dubiae efficiatur, et certa rerum intelligentia monstretur, quia fidei rerum gestarum intelligentia necessaria est: non enim sufficit credere, nisi etiam intelligatur quod creditur.

Explicit in argumentum secundum Matthaeum.

Explanatiuncula de breviariorum et capitulorum canonumque differentia

INCIPIT BREVIARIUM SECUNDUM MATTHAEUM. Nativitas Christi. Magi cum muneribus veniunt, et reliqua.

Perquirendum est quid inter breviarium et capitulum atque canonem distet. His etenim tribus, quasi quibusdam clavibus, cuncta evangelici voluminis arcana reserantur. Nam sublatis breviariis, capitulis et canonibus, omnia confusa erunt et ambigua, et quae sunt eadem, vel vicina, vel sola, et qui vel quot evangelistae in quibuslibet sententiis consonent, aut de quibus rebus edisserant, hoc totum sine praedictis clavibus amphibolum erit. Itaque haec tria propriis differentiis ab invicem discernamus. Breviarium est rerum in contextu Evangelii narratarum compendiosa et brevis expositio. Unde et breviarium brevis causa nominatur, eo quod per hoc totus Evangeliorum textus breviter comprehenditur. Capitulum est quaelibet in Evangeliis sententia seu narratio. Canon est titulus, quo cognoscitur concordia evangelistarum, id est quis, vel qui, vel quot evangelistae unumquodque capitulum ediderunt. Ob necessarias itaque causas haec tria reperta sunt. Nam breviarium ob hoc repertum est, quatenus ipsae res quae evangelico volumine narrantur, hoc breviter praemisso et considerato compendio, citius et lucidius patescant, ut quod in Evangelio quisque invenire desiderat, breviariorum consideratione cum summa facilitate reperiat. Canones ob hanc causam reperti et vocati sunt, quatenus eorum distinctione, concordia evangelistarum, id est qui et quot evangelistae eadem vel vicina vel sola in Evangeliis capitula dixerunt, agnoscatur. Capitula ob hoc inventa et notata sunt, ut per haec quaelibet sententia vel narratio in quolibet Evangelio agnoscatur. Notandum quoque quod nec capitulum sine canone, nec canon sine capitulo, per totum Evangelii contextum esse possunt, quia haec duo sibi invicem inseparabiliter connexa sunt. Licet enim fieri possit ut ex negligentia scriptorum, quodvis capitulum numerum sui canonis non habeat subscriptum, vere tamen aliquo canone carere non poterit. At breviarium sine canone vel capitulis subscriptis, licet non absque capitulorum sensu, consistit. Non enim in breviario qui vel quot evangelistae quolibet sensu ediderunt, neque capitulorum numerus perquiritur: alioquin quomodo contextui evangelico, sic et breviario, uterque numerus canonum et capitulorum superscribendo apponeretur. Quod quia non agitur, manifestum est quod illud in breviario proprie discitur, ut quae in evangelico textu diversis capitulis et canonibus multiplici narratione exponuntur, ea in breviario, quasi quodam pugillo, brevi assertione demonstrentur.

Illud quoque notandum quod sicut breviarium sine canone et capitulis consistit, sic et capitula sine breviario saepe posita reperiuntur. Nam in exordio Evangelii secundum Matthaeum, in quo ter XIV, hoc est XLII generationes describuntur, duo capitula duoque canones, tertius videlicet ac decimus canon, absque breviario includuntur. Si quidem in eo quod subsequitur, Christi autem generatio sic erat, et reliqua, initium breviarii exorditur. Nam ibi nativitas Domini exponitur. Cur autem non a principio XL et duarum generationum breviarium Evangelii secundum Matthaeum sumat exordium, investigandum est. Poterat enim tale breviarium, nulla obsistente ratione, sic constare, XL duarum generationum enumeratio, nativitas Christi, et reliqua: sed propter nativitatis Dominicae excellentiam, ab ultima, id est quadragesima secunda generatione, seu nativitate Salvatoris, exordium breviarii sumpsit. Nec mirum si in breviario sicuti quaedam in brevi colliguntur, ita nonnulla causa brevitatis omittuntur, cum utrumque breviarii sit proprium: alioquin breviarium non erit breviarium. Notandum quoque in caeteris evangelistis, quod in his quaedam capitula et canones ante initium breviarii posita reperiuntur, ut in exordiis Evangeliorum Marci, Lucae et Joannis, post quaedam capitula vel canones, initia breviariorum exordiuntur. Illud quoque sciendum est quod cum canones et capitula, aliquando in principio, aliquando in medio, nonnunquam etiam prope finem cujuslibet sensus adnotentur, breviaria nonnisi in primordialibus sensuum locis exordiuntur. Unde evenit ut ipsa breviaria saepe in principio, aliquando in medio, nonnunquam etiam prope finem capitulorum, sed tamen in principio sensuum, exordia sumant.

Explanatiuncula

Hoc argumentum genus officiumque et electionem Marci evangelistae prima sui parte declarat, secunda intentionem ejusdem evangelistae in scribendo Christi Evangelio ostendit, tertia ipsius Marci episcopatus dignitatem cum laudis praeconio describit. Postremo qualiter per singula ipsum opus evangelicum intelligere debeamus admonet. Itaque nomen et officium ipsius personae in argumenti fronte ponitur, cum Marcus evangelista ipse designatur. « Marcus evangelista: » Marcus Hebraeo sermone excelsus dicitur; evangelista Graece bona nuntians interpretatur. « Dei et Petri in baptismate filius atque in divino sermone discipulus. » Ob hoc excelsus merito et evangelista fieri promeruit, quia divina praestante gratia prius baptismate in Christo renatus, in divina sapientia instructus est. Sic autem distinguendum est, ut primo pronuntietur « Marcus evangelista, » ac deinde subinferatur: « Dei et Petri in baptismate filius. » Marcus filius Dei est in baptismate, quia baptismatis fonte in Deo renatus, per adoptionis gratiam Filius Dei efficitur. Filius Petri in baptismate esse dicitur, quia ab ipso baptizatus et instructus, recte spiritualis ejus filius nominatur. De qua re Apostolus: Filioli mei, quos iterum parturio donec formetur Christus in vobis. « Sacerdotium in Israel agens secundum carnem Levita. » Pristinum sacerdotale officium et nobilitas carnalis prosapiae ejusdem Marci ostenditur, ut non immerito ad apicem spiritualis et excellentioris sacerdotii postmodum transcenderet, qui prius carnale sacerdotium juste ac legitime in Israel agebat, cum ex Levi sacerdotali tribu ortus est. Sed quando et ubi Evangelium scripserit, demonstratur cum subditur: « conversus ad fidem Christi Evangelium in Italia scripsit. Tunc, inquit, Evangelium scripsit, postquam ad fidem Christi conversus est. Nam antequam fidem Christi perciperet, digna de Christo scribere non poterat. Locus conscribendi Evangelii Italia esse monstratur, in qua ipsum opus scriptum fuisse traditur: non quod Italico vel Romano, sed Graeco sermone, conscriptum sit.

Cur autem Marcus Evangelium scripserit, demonstratur cum subjungitur: « Ostendens in eo opere quid generi suo deberet et Christo. » Nam cum ipse Levita erat, ex qua tribu multi prophetae orti fuerant, suum Evangelium a voce prophetica rite inchoavit: et tanquam Levitam, de Joanne Baptista similiter

Levita et Altissimi propheta, ipsum oportebat prophetica voce testimonium perhibere. Quin etiam cum Christus non solum ex tribu Juda, sed ex tribu quoque Levi carnis originem duxit, ipsi Domino Leviticus evangelista debitor erat ut ejus Evangelium conscriberet. Unde subditur: « nam initium principii in voce propheticae exclamationis instituens, ordinem Leviticae electionis ostendit. » Claret namque quod beatus Marcus debitum Levitarum ministerium in opere evangelico demonstravit, dum non alibi exordium sui Evangelii quam in propheticis eloquiis instruere procuravit, et quasi bonus opifex et architectus super prophetarum fundamentum opus evangelicum construere coepit: non quod prophetae ex aliis tribubus orti non essent, sed quia praecipue Leviticae tribui secundum electionem Domini propheticum ministerium fuerat concessum. Non ergo quasi per rapinam indebitum sibi ministerium Marcus usurpavit, sed juxta electionem suae prosapiae Evangelium scribere inchoavit. Quod vero ait « initium principii, » difficile est ad intelligendum. Nam hujus argumenti repertor, usitatius dicere poterat: initium Evangelii, vel principium Evangelii: sed magis abstruse quam usitate eloqui voluit. Sciendum est itaque hanc distantiam esse inter principium et initium, quod principium plures in se sententias comprehendit, initium autem pars est principii, id est quaelibet sententiola principalis intra ipsum principium conclusa. Ergo principium Evangelii secundum Marcum totum illud intelligamus quod in quatuor principalibus capitulis de Joanne Baptista refertur. Initium vero inchoamentum esse ipsius principii, id est propheticum illud vaticinium quod de ipso Joanne praecursore Domini quondam fuerat praedictum; hoc est quod sit angelus ante faciem Domini praemissus, et vox verbum Patris praecurrens. Cur autem in voce propheticae exclamationis, initium ipsius principii Marcus inchoaret, causa ostenditur cum subditur: « ut praedicans praedestinatum Joannem filium Zachariae, » et reliqua usque: « ostenderet. » Dum beatus Marcus Joannem praecursorem Domini praedicat, quod angelus sit ante faciem, id est, manifestam apparitionem incarnationis Christi, praemissus, et quod vox sit verbum Patris, conceptione, nativitate, doctrina, baptismate, praecurrens, ibi procul dubio non solum Verbum, id est unicum Dei Filium, carnem sumpsisse ostendit, sed et veram animam inseparabiliter habuisse declarat. Non enim juxta haereticam pravitatem, Christi divinitas solam sine anima carnem, sed totum hominem secundum corpus et animam assumpsit. In eo autem quod ait « corpus Domini in omnia per verbum divinae vocis animatum, » non aliud ibi verbum quam divinam vocem intelligere oportet, ut sit sensus, per verbum divinae vocis, per ipsum verbum, quod nihil aliud est quam divina vox. Verbum namque Patris id ipsum est et vox. Patris, per quod verbum quomodo omnia facta sunt, sic anima Christi creata est. Ob hoc namque dicitur: « corpus Domini in omnia per verbum divinae vocis animatum. » Audito itaque verbi vel vocis nomine, non nobis carnalis consuetudo obstrepat, ut tale verbum vel vocem Patris cogitemus, qualia verba sonantia et transitoria proferimus. Sed hoc melius in sequentibus advertemus.

Nam subditur. « Ut qui haec legens sciret cui, » et reliqua usque: « inveniret. » Ordo verborum est: Ut qui haec legens sciret qui deberet scire et praedicare agnoscere initium carnis in Domino, et caro, id est habitaculum Jesu advenientis; atque id se verbum vocis inveniret, quod in consonantibus scilicet aliis evangelistis perdiderat. Aptum, inquit, erat ut Marcus Levita de Domino Salvatore, qui ex Levi ortus est, scriberet, ut quisquis haec legeret principatum, ordinem et quoddam privilegium Leviticae electionis pernosceret. Nam quae congruentius quam Levitae caro, id est carnalis prosapia et origo, debuit agnoscere initium sumendae carnis in Domino vel in unitate personae Domini? Quae Salvatoris caro, quid aliud dicenda est quam Jesu in hunc mundum advenientis habitaculum, qui habitu carnis inventus est ut homo? Illis enim evangelistis qui ex Levi orti sunt, ut Matthaeus et Marcus, dignius quam caeteris, mysterium incarnationis Domini, ex Levi quoque oriundi, scribere congruebat. Aptum quoque erat ut eadem Levitica caro, vel Marcus qui carnalem originem ex tribu Levi traxerat, in se, id est in suo animo et intellectu, verbum vocis inveniret. Ubi nobis est advertendum quod quamvis Joannes Baptista vox, et Christus verbum nominetur, non tamen Christus vocis vel Joannis, sed potius Patris Verbum est vel Filius. Possumus tamen Jesum ipsum verbum vocis, Jesum incongrue dicere verbum Joannis, qui vox nominatur, quia Verbum vel Christum praeeundo praedicabat. Nam verbum vocis, verbum vel sermonem, quem vox loquitur, dicere possumus. Non quod Joannes illud verbum genuerit, sed quod tanquam vox, ipsum Verbum, vel Christum, prophetando antecesserit. Quis enim dubitet quod vox nostra prius sonat, ut postmodum verbum audiri possit?

Illud autem quod ait: « quod in consonantibus perdiderat, » quasi inextricabilis nodus esse videtur. Nam si hujus argumenti effector sic diceret, quod consonantibus prodiderat, ut esset sensus, quod Marcus hoc verbum vocis, vel sermonem Joannis, etiam aliis evangelistis simul cum Marco consonantibus, manifestaverat, facilis intelligentia esset. Sed cum non prodiderat sed perdiderat, in exemplaribus scriptum habetur, perquirendum est quomodo Marcus hoc verbum vocis in consonantibus aliis evangelistis perdiderit. An forte in ipsis hoc verbum vocis non invenerat, ut hoc sit perdere quod est non invenire? Constat namque quod mysterium incarnationis Christi Marcus Petri apostoli discipulus, tam ex prophetica quam ex apostolica doctrina perceperat. Tamen verbum divinae vocis, vel Christum, secundum deitatem Verbum esse Patris, in consonantibus evangelistis, vel Matthaeo et Luca, qui secundum quosdam, ut ecclesiastica dicit historia, ante Marcum primo sua conscripsere Evangelia, monstratum non invenerat, siquidem hoc verbi mysterium aliquando monstrandum soli Joanni tanquam altius volanti aquilae fuerat reservandum. Et cum Marcus vocem clamantis, hoc est Joannem, vocem fuisse dictum, etiam aliis evangelistis consonantibus, invenerat, Christum quoque verbum vocis, licet non in aliorum scriptis, tamen in se, id est in sua mente, procul dubio invenit. Quamvis itaque Marcus in consonantibus evangelistis, vel Matthaeo et Luca, ipsum Joannem nomine vocis nuncupatum esse invenerat, tamen verbum vocis, vel unicum Dei Filium, nomine Verbi designatum, in consonantibus evangelistis non legerat, dum neque adhuc beatus Joannes arcanum ipsius Verbi mysterium scriptis monstraverat; quod tamen Verbum in se, id est, in suo intellectu, divina revelante gratia, Marcus procul dubio invenerat. Neque enim sanctum evangelistam, qui templum Dei electum erat, mysterium verbi divinae vocis latebat, quamvis aliorum evangelistarum scriptis hoc verbum non didicerat.

Sequitur: « Denique et perfecti Evangelii opus intrans, » et reliqua usque: « protulit angelorum. » Perfectum Evangelium dicitur quod per triennium et semis post perceptum ab Joanne baptismum usque ad tempus suae passionis et resurrectionis ab ipso Domino fuerat praedicatum. Ideoque per hominis formam Marcus designatur, cum ea praecipue quae homo Christus in carne gesserat, breviter enarravit, omisso scilicet Verbi, quod est Christus, mysterio, atque carnis genealogia quam in prioribus evangelistis, id est, Matthaeo et Luca, pleniter descriptam esse agnoverat. Totus itaque dicitur vel plenus vel perfectus, quia plena et perfecta de Domino retulit. In primis dicitur, vel in principalibus Evangelii sui locis: non enim per omnia in mediis neque in ultimis locis, totus tota protulit, cum multa in quibusdam tota praetermisit, sed in primis totus haec tota breviter narravit; expositionem videlicet deserti, jejunium numeri, tentationem diaboli, congregationem bestiarum, et ministerium angelorum. Ubi notandum quare jejunium numeri, et non potius numerum jejunii dixerit, nisi quia eminentior est numerus quam jejunium. Non enim numerus propter jejunium, sed propter sacratum numerum, jejunium illud tot dierum et noctium fuerat transactum. Nam quadragenarius numerus magnum in se mysterium continet, et ab hoc illud jejunium proprii juris est ipsius quadragenarii numeri. Cur autem totus haec tota protulerit? « Ut instituens, inquit, nos ad intelligendum, » et reliqua usque: « non negaret. » Aptum namque erat ut singula Dominica gesta quasi in brevi pugillo sive tabella astringeret, quia sicut nihil est fastidiosius prolixitate, ita nihil est gratius lucida brevitate. Ut nec sic auctoritatem factae rei demeret. Auctoritatem nominat auctorale magisterium, quo ex ore Petri apostoli de dictis et factis Dominicis Marcus fuerat instructus. Ergo sicut ex magisterio Petri apostoli ipsam factam rem, id est, gestam Dominicam historiam didicit, sic decurtans, prout Spiritus sanctus ejus intellectum gubernabat, eamdem historiam litteris tradidit, et tamen de ipsis quae scripserat, tacendo et celando nihil dempserat. Sicque suo operi evangelico perficiendo plenitudinem non negavit, dum plenum opus ex omnibus quae scribere coeperat, licet brevi sermone, perfecit.

Marcum itaque ad opus evangelicum divina praedestinatione fuisse electum, et quod nulla occasione praedestinatio Domini possit impediri, attendamus in eo quod sequitur. « Denique amputasse sibi post fidem pollicem dicitur, » et reliqua usque: « episcopus fuit. » Mos fuerat Hebraici populi ut nullus inhonestam habens in corpore maculam, ad sacerdotium perveniret. Quo mystice insinuatum est ut nemo peccatorum maculis contaminatus sacerdotio dignus sit. Quod Marcus secundum litteram attendens, propter humilitatem amputavit sibi pollicem, ne fastigium melioris sacerdotii quasi jam reprobus ascenderet. Sed in eo ipso quo se indignum sacerdotio aestimavit, magis factus est dignus. Nam secundum divinam praedestinationem non utcunque sacerdos vel doctor, sed etiam praeclarissimae urbis Alexandriae episcopus exstitit, ut qui Graeco sermone Evangelium scripserat, Graecis ibidem habitantibus et cunctis Africae gentibus, quasi terrae inaquosae, divini dogmatis fluenta ministraret.

His expositis, brevis argumenti conclusio subditur: « cujus per singula opus scire, » et reliqua usque: « volumus agnosci. » His sententiolis omnibus verbum quod est volumus per zeugma subnectendum est. Ut sit sensus, cujus per singula opus scire volumus, et Evangelii in se dicta disponere volumus, et divinam in carne Dei intelligere naturam volumus, quae nos primum requiri volumus, dehinc inquisita agnosci volumus. Quod vero ait, disciplinam legis nos in Marco agnoscere, tam propheticas sententias quam testimonia ex divina lege sumpta, ubicunque in Evangelio Marci introducuntur, non incongrue accipimus. Saepe namque nomine legis et Mosaica lex, et prophetia, et psalmus, designantur. Itaque hujus argumenti repertor pro suo labore se mercedem accepturum sperat, ita subjungens: « habentes mercedem exhortationis: qui plantat et qui rigat, unum sunt, qui autem incrementum praestat, Deus est. » Hunc sensum Apostolus ita scribit: Ego plantavi, Apollo rigavit, Deus autem incrementum dedit. Apostolus plantat, dum in vinea Dominica, vel in Christi Ecclesia, fidem radicando laborat: Apollo vero, tam baptismate quam subsequenti exhortationis doctrina, eosdem irrigat: Deus tamen incrementum fidei suis fidelibus tribuit. Ergo et qui plantat et qui rigat, unum sunt, quia id ipsum credunt, id ipsum desiderant: si quidem inquirendo, inveniendo, exhortando, docendo, veritatem apprehendere desiderabiliter exoptant. Ex quibus et unus fuit hujus argumenti repertor.

Finit in argumentum secundum Marcum.

The Scriptorium Project is the work of a small group of lay people of various apostolic churches who are interested in the preservation, transmission, and translation of the works of the early and medieval church. Our efforts are to make the works of the church fathers accessible to anyone who might have an interest in Christian antiquities and the theological, philosophical, and moral writings that have become the bedrock of Western Civilization.

To-date, our releases have pulled from the Greek, Syriac, Georgian, Latin, Celtic, Ethiopian, and Coptic traditions of Christianity, and have been pulled from sundry local traditions and languages.

Other Works from the Ancient Celtic Church Collection (Ireland, Scotland, Wales):

Three Works by Sedulius Scotus (Nov. 2007)
A Moral Interpretation by St. Aileran the Wise (Sept. 2014)
Irish Canons by Abedoc the Hibernian (Oct. 2015)
Sermons by St. Gall of Ireland (Apr. 2016)
Instructions by St. Columba of Iona (June 2017)
Lebor Gabala Erenn by Nennius the Monk (June 2017)
The Measure to be Taxed for Penance by St. Columba of Iona (Mar 2019)
Mystical Interpretation by St. Aileran the Wise (June 2020)
The Interpretation of Morals by St. Aileran the Wise (Feb. 2021)
Testament of Some Former Things by John Scotus Eriugena (Mar 2022)
The First Synod of St. Patrick by St. Patrick of Ireland (May 2022)
Of the Three Habitations by St. Patrick of Ireland (Mar 2023)

www.ingramcontent.com/pod-product-compliance
Lightning Source LLC
LaVergne TN
LVHW061043070526
838201LV00073B/5155